D1153364

700040588436

Classic Recipes of
POLAND

Classic Recipes of
POLAND

TRADITIONAL FOOD AND COOKING
IN 25 AUTHENTIC DISHES

EWA MICHALIK

LORENZ BOOKS

This edition is published by
Lorenz Books,
an imprint of Anness Publishing Ltd,
Blaby Road, Wigston, LE18 4SE

www.lorenzbooks.com;
www.annesspublishing.com

© Anness Publishing Limited 2013

If you like the images in this book and
would like to investigate using them for
publishing, promotions or advertising,
please visit our website
www.practicalpictures.com for more
information.

Publisher: Joanna Lorenz
Editor: Emma Clegg & Helen Sudell
Designer: Nigel Partridge
Production Controller: Steve Lang
Recipe Photography: Martin Brigdale

The image on the front cover is of Spiced
Red Cabbage, page 41

All rights reserved. No part of this
publication may be reproduced, stored in a
retrieval system, or transmitted in any way
or by any means, electronic, mechanical,
photocopying, recording or otherwise,
without the prior written permission of the
copyright holder.

A CIP catalogue record for this book is
available from the British Library

PUBLISHER'S NOTE
Although the advice and information in this
book are believed to be accurate and true
at the time of going to press, neither the
authors nor the publisher can accept any
legal responsibility or liability for any errors
or omissions that may have been made nor
for any inaccuracies nor for any loss, harm
or injury that comes about from following
instructions or advice in this book.

PUBLISHER'S ACKNOWLEDGEMENTS
The Publisher would like to thank the
following agencies for the use of their
images. Alamy: p10bl, p10tr, p11tr.
iStockphoto: p9

COOK'S NOTES
Bracketed terms are intended for American
readers. For all recipes, quantities are given
in both metric and imperial measures and,
where appropriate, in standard cups and
spoons. Follow one set of measures, but
not a mixture, because they are not
interchangeable.

Standard spoon and cup measures are
level. 1 tsp = 5ml, 1 tbsp = 15ml, 1 cup =
250ml/8fl oz. Australian standard
tablespoons are 20ml. Australian readers
should use 3 tsp in place of 1 tbsp for
measuring small quantities.

American pints are 16fl oz/2 cups.
American readers should use 20fl oz/2.5
cups in place of 1 pint when measuring
liquids.

Electric oven temperatures in this book are
for conventional ovens. When using a fan
oven, the temperature will probably need to
be reduced by about 10–20°C/20–40°F.
Since ovens vary, you should check with
your manufacturer's instruction book for
guidance.

The nutritional analysis given for each
recipe is calculated per portion (i.e. serving
or item), unless otherwise stated. If the
recipe gives a range, such as Serves 4–6,
then the nutritional analysis will be for the
smaller portion size, i.e. 6 servings. The
analysis does not include optional
ingredients, such as salt added to taste.

Medium (US large) eggs are used unless
otherwise stated.

Contents

Introduction

Poland sits in the very heart of Europe, surrounded on three sides by powerful neighbours, who have sought to take advantage of this rich landscape. Poland's fertile countryside abounds with all manner of good things to eat – from the northern lakes and rivers teeming with freshwater fish, and the vast central fields of wheat, to large forests inhabited by many types of animals and birds suitable for the table, and the warmer southern mountains whose foothills support farm animals including sheep, pigs and cattle. This diverse wealth of local ingredients, coupled with the techniques and ingredients brought by invading countries, gave rise to the rich and unique culinary tradition that is known and loved all over the world today.

Left: The beautiful Tatra mountains form a natural border between Slovakia and Poland.

Polish Cuisine

In a country where the people have had to battle for independence, it is a matter of national pride that the traditions of Polish cuisine have been so well preserved. Faced with bitterly cold winters, the Poles know how to make expert use of their natural resources to produce hearty and sustaining meals; Polish food is not for slimmers! The Polish toast, "Eat, drink and loosen your belt", is an indication of this serious attitude to the consumption of

Below: A typical Polish breakfast of dark rye bread, eggs and cheese with plenty of coffee.

Above: White borscht soup is a traditional Polish starter and is an alternative to red borscht.

large quantities of food. Today, the emphasis is still focused on healthy produce and excellent home cooking, where time is taken to make a meal in traditional style. Hospitality is, and has always been, highly valued – "a guest in the house is God in the house", as another Polish saying goes.

Poles start their day well with a hearty breakfast of dark rye breads, cooked meats, eggs and cheese or jam, washed down with strong tea or coffee. The main meal of the day is lunch, where traditionally people would return home for a

sustaining three-course meal. The first course of this meal is nearly always soup. The famous soup, borscht, based on the beautiful ruby-red colour of beetroot (beet), is a favourite dish. Next comes the main dish, perhaps Hunter's Stew or Pork Cutlets served with sauerkraut and other vegetables. Finally, the Poles love their desserts and will often find room for a cake such as Poppy Seed Cake or a tantalizing pastry like Plum Pudding with ice cream. Supper time tends to be a simpler affair when family gather together to take a lighter meal to conclude their day.

Apart from the three main meals of the day, many Poles have a sweet tooth and enjoy eating snacks. Many of these delicacies are based on yeast dough, for example doughnuts, or jam puffs, plum cake and pastry tarts topped with soft cheese, honey, jam or nuts.

Right: Poles enjoy nothing more than snacking on a pastry bought from a street stall.

Polish Festivals

Many of the festivals celebrated in Poland are linked to the rituals of the Catholic church and the rhythm of the Catholic calendar, with its emphasis on Christmas and Easter. These two major Christian celebrations are marked with quite magnificent seriousness in Poland, even in these days of commercialism, and the religious basis is never forgotten. Other, more pagan celebrations are also noted during the year, including hunting feasts in rural areas and

Below: The Christmas market at Rynek Glowny, Krakow.

name day parties everywhere, as well as weddings and christenings. All provide a chance for the family to enjoy themselves, but it's at Christmas and Easter that Polish people pull out all the stops with elaborate feasts and parties.

Christmas

Celebrations start early in Poland, with St Nicholas arriving on his sleigh on 6th December to hand out presents of honey and almond cookies and apples to the children. Christmas markets are very popular, selling decorations and festive foods,

Above: Honey cookies are a traditional Christmas treat.

such as smoked cheeses from the Tatra mountains. After a few weeks' wait the biggest celebration of the year on Christmas Eve (*Wigilia*) takes place. Wigilia means "waiting", and it's the anticipation of Christ's birth that is all-important. This is a huge affair of long meals and family rituals involving dressing the tree and opening gifts. This Christmas Eve meal is a major event in the Polish calendar. No meat is eaten, and people even try to avoid using animal fats in the cooking. In past years, the feast was a huge affair of twelve courses (to represent the twelve

apostles), but nowadays three or four courses are more usual.

First, the family and guests will break and share a plate of *oplatek*, the thin wafers associated with the communion service in church. There then follows a warming beetroot (beet) or sweet almond soup and some dishes of vegetables, such as sauerkraut, stuffed kohlrabi, mushrooms and potatoes. The main dish is usually a magnificent whole carp or pike and the meal ends with a dried fruit compote, and then the special Christmas pudding, *kutia*, made from wheat grains,

Below: The Easter cake is shaped to look like the folds of an old woman's skirt.

honey, poppy seeds, cherry jam, dried fruit and nuts. Those who are still hungry might nibble the traditional honey cookies, and the grown-ups can open their presents with a glass or two of fiery flavoured vodka to hand. Christmas day is a quieter affair where the family may sit down to eat a roast turkey or continue to enjoy the left-overs from the mighty Wigilia feast.

Easter

It's hard to know how to top the festivities of Wigilia, but Polish people certainly try to go one better at Easter (*Wielkanoc*), when this most important Christian festival is celebrated with lavish feasting and partying alongside the religious ritual. On Good Friday a simple meal will be prepared such as soused herrings and potatoes. Easter Saturday is spent in anticipation of the great Easter Sunday feast. In the centre of the Easter Sunday table there is often a white lamb made of sugar or butter, usually standing on a little hill of greenery made of cress.

Above: Polish girls in national costume at an Easter festival.

Once the family has gathered, a plate of quartered hard-boiled eggs is passed around and the feast can begin. This consists of cold meats, vegetables and salads; *mazurki*, the sweet, decorated pastries; and the Easter cake known as *babka*.

There are many other secular occasions throughout the year, such as weddings, and hunting festivals where people gather together to celebrate with a feast, involving a good spread of whatever food is in season.

Classic Ingredients

Poland's position on the cusp of the trade routes between eastern and western Europe means that Polish cooks have had access to a fantastic variety of home-grown ingredients. The typical central European climate of variable, humid summers and wet, cold winters gives ideal growing conditions for many seasonal crops, resulting in a natural abundance of locally

Below: The fast-flowing rivers of Poland are full of freshwater fish such as carp and pike.

grown produce. What is more, Poland's forests, rivers and lakes provide a wonderful bounty of wild foods, such as game, mushrooms and freshwater fish, which are transformed in Polish kitchens up and down the country into a wide range of inspiring recipes.

Meat, poultry and game
Pork is the main meat in Poland with every part of the pig being consumed. The pork sausage, *kielbasa*, is very important in Polish cuisine and has travelled

Above: Wild pigeon is a popular game bird both to hunt and eat.

the world with emigrating families. Poles love veal, especially the cutlets which they eat in the same way as pork chops, fried in breadcrumbs. Beef tends to be marinated and slow-cooked for hearty stews. Chicken is staple fare in Poland; however, the stronger flavours of goose and turkey are favoured for special occasions, such as Easter. Hunting is a popular pastime and there are plenty of traditional recipes for partridge, pheasant, quail, pigeon and wild duck.

Right: The Poles are adept in foraging for wild mushrooms.

Above: Sausages can be served in slices or added to stews.

Freshwater fish and seafood

Carp is bred in the lakes of northern Poland and has become a staple dish of the Christmas table and a favourite choice in restaurants where it can be freshly cooked in broth, fried in breadcrumbs or jellied in aspic. Pike is traditionally accompanied by chopped hard-boiled eggs and dressed with fresh parsley. Trout, salmon, sturgeon and perch are all plentiful in Poland's rivers and are easy and quick to cook. Haddock, sardines and halibut can be found in the Baltic sea and make fabulous dishes.

Dairy produce

Sour cream is added to all kinds of soups and stews and makes a lovely sauce with chopped hard-boiled eggs and mustard. Often made from sheep's milk, cheese is sold smoked or as curd cheese. Polish cheesecake (*sernik*), made with curd cheese, eggs, lemon and vanilla is very popular. As well as being used in baking, eggs are commonly hard-boiled, chopped and used as a garnish.

Below: Carp is a key feature of the Christmas feast.

Above: Curd cheese is used in a range of desserts.

Vegetables

The prized vegetable among Poles is beetroot (beet). They love its dark red colour and it features in many Polish dishes including the hot soup (*barszcz*). Another popular root vegetable is the humble potato which has many uses in Polish cooking. The Poles also grow and eat carrots, kohlrabi, onions and any other vegetables that can be stored for use during the cold winter months. Cabbages are preserved in brine to make sauerkraut which is used as a stuffing for dumplings (*pierogi*) and as a tasty addition to soup. Another staple of the Polish

Above: Vivid beetroots (beet) are used to make borscht.

kitchen are the mushrooms, such as chanterelles, that grow wild in the forests of Poland. Their strong, earthy flavour goes well with robust Polish dishes such as wild boar casserole.

Below: Aromatic poppy seeds are added to desserts.

Grains

Buckwheat, wheat, millet, barley and rye are grown on the flat arable fields of central Poland. The porridge-like dish, *kasza*, is made from grains simmered in water, with the addition of honey for a sweet dish, or bacon fat and salt to make it a savoury and filling accompaniment for the meat course.

Seasonings

Juniper berries, paprika, cinnamon and cloves are all used to enhance meaty casseroles and roasts. Poppy seeds and vanilla add sweetness to pastries and fresh herbs, notably dill, parsley, chives and bay leaves, add fragrance to fish dishes.

Fruit

Fresh and dried fruits abound in the Polish diet. Delectable seasonal fruits – raspberries, strawberries, peaches, plums, apples, pears, grapes – can be eaten as they are, made into delicious desserts with the addition of honey or sugar, or

Above: Dill and other fresh herbs add pungency to many stews.

included in cakes and pastries. They are also mixed with spices and sour cream to make fruit soup, dried and added to marinades for game, and soaked to make a fruit drink.

Below: Plums are a popular addition to cakes and pastries.

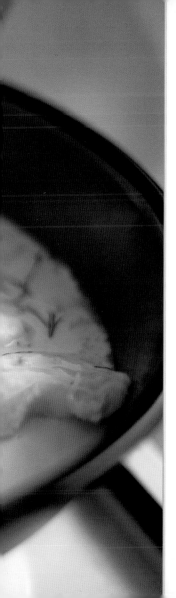

Food from the Heart

From its rolling lowlands and meandering rivers to its lofty peaks and fertile Baltic coast, Poland is a land rich in natural resources. Staple ingredients such as cereals, fish, pork, game and seasonal fruit are lovingly prepared using age-old techniques to produce wholesome, hearty and rustic dishes that satisfy both body and soul. From warming soups and tasty appetizers to comforting meat casseroles and delicious desserts, cakes and bakes, this special collection of authentic recipes aims to capture the essence of Polish food and cooking.

Left: Fresh herbs added to simmering fish gives a touch of delicacy and will enliven the dish.

Sorrel Soup with Eggs
Zupa szczawiowa z jajkiem

1 Melt the butter in a large pan, then add the chopped sorrel leaves and a pinch of salt.

2 Cook the sorrel gently over a low heat for 5–7 minutes, until the leaves have just wilted.

3 Put the flour in a small bowl and gradually add 60ml/4 tbsp stock, mixing constantly to make a paste. Add to the pan and stir to combine.

4 Stir in the remaining stock, bring to the boil and simmer for 10 minutes.

5 Season to taste with salt and ground black pepper, then gradually add the sour cream, whisking well between each addition.

6 Transfer the soup to warmed soup bowls and top with a spoonful of chopped hard-boiled egg.

VARIATION

If you are unable to find sorrel leaves, you could use rocket (arugula) or large basil leaves, although this will alter the flavour.

Serves 4

15ml/1 tbsp butter
400g/14oz fresh sorrel leaves, chopped
15ml/1 tbsp plain (all-purpose) flour
1 litre/1¾ pints/4 cups beef or vegetable stock
45–60ml/3–4 tbsp sour cream
4 hard-boiled eggs, chopped
salt and ground black pepper, to taste

Sorrel grows wild in grassy areas in Poland, but it is also cultivated commercially for use in a range of dishes, including soups, sauces and salads. It has a pleasant, slightly sour taste, which is complemented by the richness of the sour cream and hard-boiled eggs in this dish.

Red Borscht Soup Czerwony Barszcz

1 Cut the beetroot (beets), carrots and celery into fairly thick strips. Melt the butter in a large pan and cook the onions over a low heat for 5 minutes, stirring occasionally.

2 Add the beetroot, carrots and celery and cook for a further 5 minutes, stirring occasionally.

3 Add the garlic and chopped tomatoes to the pan and cook, stirring, for 2 more minutes.

4 Place the bay leaf, parsley, cloves and peppercorns in a piece of muslin and tie with string.

5 Add the muslin bag to the pan with the stock. Bring to the boil, reduce the heat, cover and simmer for 1¼ hours, or until the vegetables are very tender. Discard the bag. Stir in the beetroot *kvas* and season.

6 Heat gently until the borscht just boils, then remove from the heat. Ladle into bowls and serve with the chopped boiled eggs and soured cream, garnished with chives or dill.

COOK'S TIP
Beetroot kvas, fermented beetroot juice, adds an intense colour and a slight tartness. If unavailable, peel and grate 1 beetroot, add 150ml/¼ pint/⅔cup stock and 10ml/2 tsp lemon juice. Bring to the boil, cover and leave for 30 minutes. Strain before using. You could also use the liquid from a jar of pickled beetroot if you prefer.

Borscht made with red beetroot has been an intrinsic part of Polish cuisine for centuries. There are two versions: borscht for the Christmas Eve feast, and this one for Easter made with fermented juice.

Serves 4–6

900g/2 lb uncooked beetroot (beets), peeled

2 carrots, peeled

2 celery sticks

40g/1⁄2oz/3 tbsp butter

2 onions, sliced

2 garlic cloves, crushed

4 tomatoes, peeled, seeded and chopped

1 bay leaf

1 large parsley sprig

2 cloves

4 whole pepperorns

1.2 litres/2 pints/5 cupes beef or chicken stock

150ml/¼ pint/⅔ cup beetroot *kvas* (see cook's tip)

3 hard-boiled eggs, chopped, to garnish

100ml/3½ fl oz/scant ½ cup sour cream, to serve

chopped fresh chives or dill, to serve

Potato Pancakes Placki ziemniaczane

Serves 4–6

4–5 large potatoes, peeled and
grated
1 large onion, grated
2 eggs
60ml/4 tbsp plain (all-purpose) flour
salt and ground black pepper
(optional)
120ml/4fl oz/½ cup melted bacon fat
or oil
sour cream and paprika, or sugar, or
apple sauce to serve

1 Rinse the grated potatoes and onion, then squeeze in your hands to remove the excess liquid.

2 Put the potatoes and onion in a large bowl with the eggs, flour, and salt and pepper if serving with a savoury topping. Mix with your hands to combine thoroughly.

3 Put the bacon fat or oil in a large, heavy frying pan and heat over a high heat until it is almost smoking.

4 Carefully put a large spoonful of the potato mixture into the pan and flatten it slightly with a fork. Repeat until you have about four pancakes in the pan.

5 Fry each pancake until it is golden brown on both sides, then remove from the pan with a slotted spoon and drain on kitchen paper.

6 Keep the cooked pancakes warm in a low oven while you cook the rest of the mixture in the same way.

7 Serve the pancakes warm, with a topping of your choice.

This dish was especially popular during World War II, when there was little to buy in the shops, and it was served as a treat for children. Today, these pancakes are still eaten, and taste delicious with sugar, apple sauce, or a dollop of sour cream and a dash of paprika.

Grilled Sardines with Parsley
Sardynki z rusztu z pietruszką

Serves 4

900g/2lb fresh sardines, gutted and
    scaled
30ml/2 tbsp melted butter or
    vegetable oil
salt and ground black pepper, to taste
60ml/4 tbsp chopped fresh parsley,
    to garnish
lemon wedges, to serve

Sardines are easy to cook, good value for money and extremely tasty, so it is little wonder that they are popular in Poland. Here, they are simply grilled and served with lemon wedges to squeeze over. This recipe also works well on a barbecue.

1 Preheat the grill (broiler) to high. Wash the prepared sardines under cold running water and pat dry on kitchen paper.

2 Brush the fish with melted butter or oil, then season to taste with salt and pepper.

3 Place the sardines on the grill pan and put under the preheated grill. Cook for about 3–4 minutes on each side, until the skin begins to brown.

4 Transfer the sardines to warmed plates, sprinkle with parsley, and serve immediately with lemon wedges.

Halibut Steaks with Lemon Butter
Steak halibuta z masłem cytrynowym

Serves 4

4 halibut steaks, about 185g/6½oz
    each
salt and ground black pepper, to taste
150g/5oz/10 tbsp butter, softened
30ml/2 tbsp chopped fresh parsley
30ml/2 tbsp lemon juice
lemon wedges, to serve
parsley sprigs, to garnish (optional)

1 Preheat the grill (broiler) to medium. Season the fish with salt and pepper on both sides.

2 Mix together the butter, parsley and lemon juice, then spread over both sides of each fish steak.

3 Line a grill pan with foil, then put the steaks on the foil. Place under the grill and cook for 7–8 minutes on each side, until tender.

4 Transfer to warmed plates. Serve immediately, with lemon wedges for squeezing over, and garnished with parsley sprigs if using.

Poles often simply grill or fry fresh fish, and this elegant dish is a good example. Spreading the steaks with parsley, lemon and butter before cooking ensures the flesh is moist and enables the aromas to permeate the fish without overpowering its delicate flavour.

Fried Carp in Breadcrumbs
Karp smażony

1 First scald the carp by putting it into a large heatproof dish or roasting pan and pouring boiling water over it. Turn and repeat on the other side. Drain well.

2 Cut the cleaned and scalded carp into even-sized portions and sprinkle lightly with salt. Leave to stand for about 30 minutes. Remove the skin, if you like.

3 Mix together the flour and pepper in a medium bowl. Put the beaten egg in another, and the breadcrumbs in a third.

4 Dip the fish pieces first into the flour, then into the egg, then into the breadcrumbs, coating them evenly at each stage.

5 Heat the oil in a large, heavy pan, until very hot. Carefully add the coated fish pieces and cook for about 5 minutes on each side, until golden brown all over.

6 Remove the fish pieces using a slotted spoon and drain on kitchen paper. Serve with lemon wedges.

Serves 4

1 carp, about 900g/2lb, cleaned and
   filleted
2.5ml/½ tsp salt
50g/2oz/½ cup plain (all-purpose)
   flour
pinch ground black pepper
1–2 eggs, lightly beaten
115g/4oz/1¾ cups dry breadcrumbs
90ml/6 tbsp vegetable oil, for frying
lemon wedges, to serve

This farmhouse dish is the main course of the traditional 12-course Christmas Eve feast, but it makes a delicious meal at any time of the year and it is very straightforward to do. Chunks of carp are coated in breadcrumbs and fried in oil, and served simply with lemon wedges.

Chicken Casserole
Potrawka z kurczaka

1 Strain the mushrooms, reserving the juices, then chop finely. Put the chicken in a flameproof casserole, add the water and bring to the boil. Simmer for 10 minutes.

2 Add the mushrooms, celery, carrot, parsley and reserved mushroom juices to the casserole. Season, then cover and simmer for 30–45 minutes.

3 Meanwhile, make the roux. Melt the butter in a small pan, add the flour and cook, stirring, for 1 minute.

4 Remove the chicken from the casserole with a slotted spoon and set aside on a warm plate. Add the roux to the casserole and stir. Add the wine and bring to the boil.

5 Remove the casserole from the heat. Put the egg yolks in a small bowl and add a ladleful of the hot juices, stirring constantly. Add to the casserole and stir to combine.

6 Return the chicken to the sauce and heat gently to warm through. Serve with Buckwheat Kasha.

COOK'S TIP
To get the full, authentic flavour of this traditional casserole, it's best to use organic chicken.

Serves 4

50g/2oz dried mushrooms, rinsed and soaked in warm water for 30 minutes
800g/1¾lb chicken pieces
550ml/18fl oz/2½ cups water
2 celery stalks, chopped
1 carrot, chopped
30ml/2 tbsp chopped fresh parsley
25g/1oz/2 tbsp butter
25g/1oz/2 tbsp plain (all-purpose) flour
120ml/4fl oz/½ cup dry white wine
2 egg yolks
salt and ground black pepper, to taste
Buckwheat Kasha (see page 46), to serve

Warming and nourishing, this casserole is ideal comfort food during cold weather. Served with Buckwheat Kasha it makes a delicious and sustaining main meal.

Roast Duck with Fruit Stuffing
Kaczka z owocami

Serves 4

1 large duck, about 2.75kg/6lb
3 apples, chopped
2 whole oranges, chopped
12 prunes, chopped
12 fresh or dried apricots, chopped
175ml/6fl oz/¾ cup fresh orange
   juice
30ml/2 tbsp clear honey
Spiced Red Cabbage (see page 41),
   to serve

For the marinade

juice of 1 lemon
5ml/1 tsp dried marjoram
salt and ground black pepper, to taste

1 Wash the duck and pat dry with kitchen paper, then put it into a large dish.

2 Mix the marinade ingredients together in a small bowl, then rub over the duck. Cover and leave to marinate for 2 hours, or overnight.

3 Preheat the oven to 180°C/350°F/Gas 4. Mix together the apples, oranges, prunes, apricots, orange juice and honey, then stuff into the cavity.

4 Weigh the duck and calculate the cooking time: allow 20 minutes per 500g/1¼lb, plus an extra 20 minutes.

5 Place the duck in a roasting pan and roast for the calculated time. To test whether it is cooked, pierce the thickest part with a knife; the juices should run clear.

6 Cover with foil and allow it to rest for about 15 minutes. Remove the fruit from the cavity and carve the meat.

7 Transfer the meat to a serving platter and arrange the fruit around it. Serve with Spiced Red Cabbage.

COOK'S TIP
Duck is a fatty bird, so it is best roasted with a stuffing that will cut through the fat, such as this fresh, fruity one.

Duck is considered a luxury in Poland, and is usually reserved for special occasions. Often, as in this recipe, it is roasted and served with a range of different fruits.

Wild Boar with Sweet-and-sour Sauce
Cząber z dzika

Serves 4–6

1 piece wild boar rump, about
  2kg/4½lb
115g/4oz/⅔ cup lard
30ml/2 tbsp plain (all-purpose) flour
15ml/1 tbsp rosehip preserve
5ml/1 tsp ground cinnamon
5ml/1 tsp sugar
5ml/1 tsp salt
redcurrant jelly, to serve

For the marinade

500ml/17fl oz/2¼ cups water
500ml/17fl oz/2¼ cups dry red wine
90ml/6 tbsp vinegar
2 strips of lemon rind
2 onions, sliced
3 large garlic cloves, chopped
1 carrot, chopped
½ celeriac, chopped
1 parsnip, chopped
15 prunes
10 black peppercorns
10 allspice berries, cracked
4–5 whole cloves
20 juniper berries
4 bay leaves
1 piece fresh root ginger, chopped

1 Place all the marinade ingredients in a stainless steel pan and bring to the boil. Simmer for 5 minutes, then cool. Add the meat, cover, place in the refrigerator and chill. Leave to marinate for 3–4 days.

2 Preheat the oven to 180°C/350°F/Gas 4. Heat the lard in a flameproof casserole. Add the meat and brown all over. Scoop out the vegetables and lemon from the marinade and add to the meat in the casserole.

3 Strain the marinade. Add to the casserole. Cook for 2 hours. Lift out the meat, cover and rest for 15 minutes.

4 Mix together the flour, rosehip preserve, cinnamon, sugar and salt, then add to the casserole. Stir to mix and return to the oven for 10 minutes.

5 Carve the meat into slices, then transfer to plates and spoon over the sauce. Serve with redcurrant jelly.

Harking back to ancient days when hunters caught wild boar in the forests around Poland, this old Polish recipe involves marinating the tender rump for several days before roasting and serving it with a flavoursome sauce.

Roast Beef Roll Zrazy

Serves 4–6

1.3kg/3lb piece boneless rump steak
25g/1oz/2 tbsp butter
120ml/4fl oz/½ cup beef stock
pinch of salt
Buckwheat Kasha (see page 46) and
   a green salad, to serve

For the stuffing

50g/2oz/⅓ cups dried mushrooms,
   soaked in warm water for 30
   minutes
25g/1oz streaky (fatty) smoked bacon
15g/½oz/1 tbsp butter
1/2 onion, finely chopped
15ml/1 tbsp fresh breadcrumbs
1 egg, beaten
15ml/1 tbsp sour cream
15ml/1 tbsp chopped fresh parsley
salt and ground black pepper, to taste

*This traditional Polish dish is
a combination of fine steak
and strong-flavoured
mushrooms. Stuffed meat
dishes have been a part of
Polish cooking since the
17th century, and are often
served on festive occasions.*

1 To make the stuffing, strain the mushrooms and put into a food processor with the bacon. Process to a paste, then scrape into a bowl.

2 Heat the butter in a pan, then add the onion and fry for 5 minutes. Leave to cool, then add to the mushrooms with the breadcrumbs, egg, sour cream, parsley and seasoning. Knead to combine.

3 Using a mallet, pound the steak to the thickness of your little finger. Spread the stuffing all over the meat, then roll tightly. Tuck the edges in and tie with scalded white cotton thread.

4 Heat the butter in a large pan. Sprinkle the roll with salt, then add to the pan and seal on all sides. Add the stock and simmer for 30 minutes. Place a roasting pan in the oven and preheat to 180°C/350°F/Gas 4. Transfer the beef roll and the juices to the pan and roast for 30 minutes. Check the meat occasionally and add more stock if required.

5 Remove the thread and cut into thin slices. Ladle over the juices and serve with Buckwheat Kasha and a green salad.

Breaded Pork Cutlets Kotlet schabowy

Serves 4

4 boneless pork cutlets, fat on, each
   weighing about 225g/8oz
2.5ml/½ tsp salt
2.5ml/½ tsp ground black pepper
115g/4oz/1 cup plain (all-purpose)
   flour
2 eggs, beaten
65g/2½oz/1 cup fine fresh
   breadcrumbs
1 tbsp each of chopped fresh
   rosemary, dill and sage
75ml/5 tbsp vegetable oil
fresh parsley sprigs, to garnish
lemon wedges, mashed potato and
   sauerkraut or red cabbage, to
   serve

*Easy to make and quick to
cook, this recipe for pork
cutlets dipped in
breadcrumbs and simply
fried is particularly popular
all over Poland.*

1 Cut slits in the rind of the pork cutlets to prevent them from curling
during cooking. Using a meat mallet, rolling pin or the base of a frying
pan, pound each cutlet lightly on each side to flatten, then sprinkle each
side with salt and pepper.

2 Put the flour and beaten eggs in separate bowls. In another bowl,
mix the breadcrumbs with the chopped herbs.

3 Dip the cutlets first in the flour, then the egg and then into the
breadcrumb mixture.

4 Heat the oil in a frying pan, then add the breaded pork and fry on a
high heat for 4–5 minutes on each side, until golden brown all over.

5 Reduce the heat and cook for a further 2 minutes to ensure the pork
is cooked all the way through.

6 Garnish with parsley and serve immediately with mashed potato and
sauerkraut or red cabbage, and with lemon wedges for squeezing over.

Serves 6–8

1kg/2¼ lb fresh cabbage, finely
　shredded
10 dried mushrooms (boletus)
2 onions, chopped
500g/1¼ lb smoked sausage, sliced
1kg/2¼ lb sauerkraut, drained
2 cooking apples, peeled, cored and
　diced
10 prunes
10 juniper berries, crushed
3–4 bay leaves
10 peppercorns
2.5ml/½ tsp salt
750ml/1¼ pints/3 cups boiling water
500g/1¼ lb roast pork, diced
500g/1¼ lb roast beef, diced
500g/1¼ lb boiled ham, diced
150ml/¼ pint/⅔ cup dry red wine
5ml/1 tsp honey
wholemeal (whole-wheat) or rye
　bread and chilled vodka, to serve

Hunter's Stew Bigos

1 Place the cabbage in a heatproof colander and wilt the leaves by carefully pouring boiling water over it.

2 Rinse the mushrooms, then place them in a bowl with enough warm water to cover. Leave to soak for 15 minutes, then transfer to a pan and cook in the soaking liquid for 30 minutes. Strain, reserving the cooking liquid, then cut the mushrooms into strips.

3 Put the onions and smoked sausage in a small frying pan and fry gently, until the onions have softened. Remove the sausage from the pan and set aside.

4 Put the wilted cabbage and drained sauerkraut in a large pan, then add the cooked onions, along with the mushrooms, mushroom cooking liquid, apples, prunes, juniper berries, bay leaves, peppercorns and salt. Pour over the boiling water, then cover and simmer gently for 1 hour.

5 Add the cooked sausage to the pan with the other cooked, diced meats. Pour in the wine and add the honey.

6 Cook, uncovered, for a further 40 minutes, stirring frequently. Taste and adjust the seasoning as required. Remove from the heat.

7 Allow the stew to cool, then cover it and transfer to the refrigerator. Leave it overnight. Return to the boil and simmer for 10 minutes to heat through. Serve with wholemeal or rye bread and a glass of chilled vodka.

Considered by some to be the national dish, bigos is one of the most treasured of the old Polish recipes. Hearty and sustaining, this sauerkraut, cabbage and meat stew can be found in many different forms throughout Poland. It is usually allowed to cool and then reheated several times so that the flavours can intensify. Start preparing it a day in advance.

Stuffed Cabbage Rolls Gołąbki

1 To make the stuffing, bring a large pan of lightly salted water to the boil and cook the rice, according to the instructions on the packet. Once the grains are tender, drain and rinse under cold water to prevent them from cooking further.

2 Drain the mushrooms and chop them finely. Heat half the butter in a large pan, then add the onion and fry gently until golden brown.

3 Add the pork, beef, garlic, mushrooms and seasoning. Cook, stirring, until the meat is browned all over, then remove from the heat and leave to cool slightly.

4 Bring a large pan of lightly salted water to the boil and cook the whole cabbage for 10–15 minutes, or until you can insert a knife into the centre easily, but the leaves are not too soft. Lift the cabbage out of the water and leave to cool slightly.

5 Preheat the oven to 190°C/375°F/Gas 5. Add the egg, nutmeg and parsley to the meat mixture and stir to combine well.

6 When it is cool enough to handle, separate the cabbage into individual leaves. Use the tough outside leaves to line an ovenproof dish. Drizzle over the oil.

7 Place a spoonful of the meat mixture in the centre of each of the remaining cabbage leaves, fold over the edges and roll to form a tight package.

8 Arrange the rolls in a single layer on the oiled cabbage leaves in the dish. Pour over the tomatoes and boiling water, and dot the remaining butter over the top. Cover the dish with a lid or foil.

9 Cook in the preheated oven for about 1 hour, or until the rolls are tender. Serve immediately, with spoonfuls of the tomato sauce.

Serves 4

1 small cabbage
10ml/2 tsp vegetable oil
400g/14oz can chopped tomatoes
60ml/4 tbsp boiling water
salt and ground black pepper, to taste

For the stuffing

100g/33/4oz/½ cup long grain rice
15g/1/2oz/¼ cup dried wild
    mushrooms, rinsed and soaked in
    warm water for 30 minutes
15ml/1 tbsp butter
½ large onion, finely chopped
225g/8oz/1 cup minced (ground) pork
225g/8oz/1 cup minced (ground) beef
1 garlic clove, finely chopped
1 small (US medium) egg, beaten
2.5ml/½ tsp freshly grated nutmeg
10ml/2 tsp chopped fresh parsley

Golabki, meaning "little pigeons", are one of the most popular dishes in Poland. Simple to prepare, cheap and very tasty, they can be made ahead in large quantities and reheated.

Sautéed Wild Mushrooms Duszone grzyby

Serves 4

450g/1lb/6½ cups fresh wild
   mushrooms
60ml/4 tbsp butter
2 large onions, halved and sliced
15ml/1 tbsp plain (all-purpose) flour
250ml/8fl oz/1 cup sour cream
salt and ground black pepper, to taste
15ml/1 tbsp chopped fresh parsley,
   to garnish

*Poland is the largest
producer of wild
mushrooms in Europe, and
collecting them is a
common pastime. This
recipe of fried onions and
mushrooms in a sour cream
sauce allows the earthy
flavours to shine through,
and can be served as an
accompaniment to fried or
roasted meat.*

1 Brush the wild mushrooms to remove any grit and wash the caps only briefly if necessary. Dry the mushrooms with kitchen paper and slice them thinly.

2 Melt the butter in a large frying pan, then add the onions. Cook gently for 5 minutes, or until they begin to brown slightly. Stir in the flour and sour cream.

3 Add the sliced mushrooms and season to taste. Simmer gently over a low heat for 15 minutes.

4 Garnish with chopped parsley and serve immediately.

Spiced Red Cabbage Czerwona kapusta

Serves 4–6

1 tbsp butter
1 large onion, sliced
1 red cabbage, finely shredded
2 cooking apples, peeled, cored and
    cut into cubes
7.5ml/1½ tsp caraway seeds
4–5 bay leaves
5–6 allspice berries
30ml/2 tbsp clear honey
juice of 1 lemon
1 glass dry red wine
6 whole cloves
salt and ground black pepper, to taste
chopped chives or parsley, to garnish

1 Melt the butter in a large frying pan over a medium heat.

2 Add the sliced onion to the frying pan and fry gently for 5 minutes, or until the onion has softened and is golden brown.

3 Put the shredded cabbage in a large, heavy pan, and pour over 1 litre/1¾ pints/4 cups boiling water.

4 Add the onion to the cabbage with the remaining ingredients. Stir well and cover. Cook over a medium heat for 15–20 minutes.

5 Check the mixture towards the end of the cooking time. The cabbage should be tender, the apples should have broken down and the liquid should have reduced by about half. If there is too much liquid, cook uncovered for a further 5 minutes.

6 Add salt and ground black pepper to taste, if you wish.

7 Serve immediately, garnished with chopped chives or parsley.

Red cabbage is one of the staples of Polish cooking. Here, it is braised with apples and aromatic spices and makes the perfect accompaniment to goose or duck.

Potato and Cheese Dumplings Pierogi

Serves 4–6

500g/1¼ lb plain (all-purpose) flour,
    plus extra for dusting
2.5ml/½ tsp salt
2 eggs, beaten
45ml/3 tbsp vegetable oil
250ml/8fl oz/1 cup warm water
chopped fresh parsley, to garnish
thick sour cream, to serve

For the filling

15g/½oz/1 tbsp butter
½ large onion, finely chopped
250g/9oz peeled, cooked potatoes
250g/9oz/1¼ cups curd (farmer's)
    cheese
1 egg, beaten
salt and ground black pepper, to taste

*Originating from old Slavic
folk cuisine, pierogi are
popular all over Poland.
They can be filled with a
number of different stuffings,
including meat and onion,
mushrooms and cabbage,
blueberries, sweet cherries,
or, as here, with potato and
curd cheese.*

1 To make the filling, heat the butter in a small pan, add the onion and cook for about 5 minutes, or until softened.

2 Push the cooked potatoes through a ricer, or mash in a large bowl. Add the cheese and stir to combine thoroughly. Add the egg, onion and seasoning to taste to the potato mixture and mix well.

3 To make the dough, sift the flour into a large bowl, then add the salt and the two eggs. Pour in the oil and water, and mix to form a loose dough.

4 Turn out on to a floured surface and knead well for about 10 minutes, or until the dough is pliant and does not stick to the work surface or your hands.

5 Divide the dough into four equal pieces, then roll each one out thinly with a floured rolling pin. (Cover the portions you are not working with with a dish towel to prevent them from drying out.) Cut the dough into 5–6cm/2–2½in circles using a pastry (cookie) cutter.

6 Place a heaped teaspoonful of the cheese filling mixture in the centre of each of the circles of dough, then fold over the dough and press firmly to seal the edges. The dumplings should be neat and well filled, but not bursting.

7 Bring a large pan of lightly salted water to the boil, add the dumplings and cook for about 4–5 minutes, or until they rise to the surface.

8 Cook for a further 2 minutes, until they have risen, then remove with a slotted spoon and place in a warmed serving dish. Garnish with chopped parsley and serve with thick sour cream.

COOK'S TIP

The dumplings can be served immediately after they are cooked, or allowed to cool and then fried in a little butter. Replace the curd cheese with cream cheese, if you prefer.

Mashed Potato Dumplings
Kopytka

1 Cut the potatoes into quarters. Place in a pan of boiling water and cook for 10–15 minutes, or until tender. Remove from the heat, drain and leave to cool.

2 Push the potatoes through a ricer, or mash to a paste with a potato masher. Add the flour, egg and salt, and knead to combine.

3 Transfer the dough to a lightly floured surface and, with damp hands, shape into walnut-sized balls. Flatten the balls slightly and make a small indentation in the centre.

4 Bring a large pan of lightly salted water to the boil, then drop in the dumplings and cook for 5 minutes, or until they are firm to the touch.

5 Meanwhile, melt the butter in a frying pan, add the breadcrumbs and fry for about 3 minutes, or until the breadcrumbs are brown.

6 Drain the dumplings and arrange on a serving dish. Sprinkle the browned breadcrumbs over the top, and serve immediately.

Serves 4–6

5 potatoes, peeled
225g/8oz/2 cups plain (all-purpose) flour
1 egg, beaten
2.5ml/½ tsp salt
45ml/3 tbsp butter
45ml/3 tbsp fresh white breadcrumbs

These soft little dumplings, which are similar to Italian gnocchi, can be served with different toppings. Here they are served with a sprinkling of crisp breadcrumbs, adding texture and colour to the dumplings. They make an excellent accompaniment to braised meats.

Buckwheat Kasha
Kasza gryczana

1 Put the buckwheat in a large, heavy pan and add the water, salt and oil or lard.

2 Bring to the boil and cook over a low heat for about 20 minutes, or until the buckwheat has absorbed all the water and the grains are soft.

3 Serve immediately.

Serves 4–6
300g/11oz/1½ cups buckwheat
500ml/17fl oz/2 ¼ cups water
pinch of salt
60ml/4 tbsp vegetable oil or
    45g/1½oz lard

COOK'S TIP
Kasha can be made with other grains, but the buckwheat version has a stronger flavour than most. It forms part of the traditional Christmas Eve supper.

Kasha has been eaten in Poland and other eastern European countries for centuries as a staple accompaniment to all kinds of roasts and stews, although it also tastes fabulous simply served with standard or soured milk.

Apple and Leek Salad Sałatka z jabłek i porów

Serves 4

2 slim leeks, white part only, washed
    thoroughly
2 large apples
15ml/1 tbsp chopped fresh parsley
juice of 1 lemon
15ml/1 tbsp clear honey
salt and ground black pepper, to taste

Fresh and tangy, this easy salad of sliced leeks and apples with a lemon and honey dressing can be served with a range of cold meats as part of a summer meal. For the best result, make sure you use slim young leeks and tart, crisp apples.

1 Thinly slice the leeks crossways. Peel and core the apples, then slice thinly.

2 Put in a large serving bowl and add the parsley, lemon juice, honey and seasoning to taste.

3 Toss well, then leave to stand in a cool place for about an hour, to allow the flavours to blend together.

COOK'S TIP
When buying leeks, look for slim ones with firm white stems and bright green leaves. Avoid those that are discoloured in any way.

Beetroot Salad Ćwikła

Serves 4–6

4–5 medium-sized raw beetroots
  (beets)
15ml/1 tbsp sugar
60–75ml/4–5 tbsp freshly grated
  horseradish
juice of 1 lemon
1 glass dry red wine
2.5ml/½ tsp salt
cold meats, to serve

*The fresh, sweet and nutty
flavour of beetroot (beet)
makes the ideal partner for
horseradish, and this salad
is often served as a side
dish with cold meats, such
as ham and Polish sausage.
Beetroot is believed to have
beauty-enhancing and
aphrodisiac properties.*

1 Put the beetroots, in their skins, in a large pan, and pour over enough water to cover.

2 Bring to the boil and cook the beetroots for about 1 hour, or until the beetroots are tender. Remove from the heat and leave to cool.

3 Peel and shred the beetroots finely. Put the shredded beetroots in a large jar with the sugar, horseradish, lemon juice, red wine and salt.

4 Cover tightly and store in a cool place for up to 4 months. Serve the beetroots with a range of cold meats.

Polish-style Cucumber Salad Mizeria

Serves 4–6

2 medium cucumbers
2.5ml/½ tsp salt
120ml/4fl oz/½ cup sour cream
juice from ½ lemon
2.5ml/½ tsp sugar (optional)
1.5ml/¼ tsp ground black pepper
15ml/1 tbsp chopped fresh chives or
   dill, to garnish

1 Peel the cucumbers, slice them thinly and place in a sieve (strainer).

2 Sprinkle over the salt, leave for a few minutes, then rinse to remove the salt and pat dry with kitchen paper.

3 To make the dressing, mix together the sour cream, lemon juice, sugar, if using, and black pepper.

4 Fold in the cucumber, then place in the refrigerator and leave for 1 hour.

5 Serve as an accompaniment, garnished with chopped chives or dill.

According to legend, this salad was a favourite dish of Queen Bona Sforza, an Italian princess who married the Polish king Sigismund I in the 16th century. Homesick for her native Italy, the dish made her cry, hence its Polish name, derived from the Latin for "misery".

Polish Cheesecake Sernik

1 Preheat the oven to 200°C/400°F/Gas 6. Grease and line a 20cm/8in round cake tin (pan).

2 Cream together the curd cheese, butter and vanilla in a large bowl until combined.

3 In a separate large bowl, whisk the egg whites with 15ml/1 tbsp sugar, until stiff peaks form.

4 In a third bowl, whisk the egg yolks with the remaining sugar until the mixture is thick and creamy.

5 Add the egg yolk and sugar mixture to the curd cheese and butter mixture with the lemon rind and stir to combine.

6 Gently fold in the egg whites, then the cornflour, semolina and raisins or sultanas, if using, taking care not to knock the air out of the mixture.

7 Transfer the mixture to the prepared tin and bake for 1 hour, or until set and golden brown.

8 Leave to cool in the tin, then dust with icing sugar and serve in slices.

COOK'S TIP

It is important to use good quality curd cheese in this recipe; it should not taste sour at all.

Serves 6–8

500g/1¼ lb/2¼ cups curd (farmer's) cheese
100g/3¾oz/scant ½ cup butter, softened
2.5ml/½ tsp vanilla extract
6 eggs, separated
150g/5oz/¾ cup caster (superfine) sugar
10ml/2 tsp grated lemon rind
15ml/1 tbsp cornflour (cornstarch)
15ml/1 tbsp semolina
50g/5oz/⅓ cup raisins or sultanas (golden raisins) (optional)
icing (confectioners') sugar, to dust

There are many versions of sernik *in Poland, which can be made with a pastry base, a cookie base or, as here in this lighter version, no base at all. It is delicious served simply with a light coating of icing sugar.*

Plum Dumplings
Knedle ze śliwkami

1 Cut the potatoes into even-sized pieces and cook in a pan of lightly salted boiling water for 10–15 minutes, or until soft. Drain, leave to cool, then mash in a large bowl.

2 Add the sour cream, 25g/1oz/2 tbsp of the butter, eggs and flour to the mashed potato and stir to combine thoroughly. Turn the dough out on to a lightly floured surface and knead lightly until the dough comes together and is firm.

3 Cut a slit down one side of each plum so that you can remove the stone (pit) while keeping the plum intact. Mix together the icing sugar and cinnamon, then push a teaspoonful into each of the plums.

4 Roll out the dough to 5mm/¼ in thick and cut into eight or twelve 10cm/4in squares (depending on how many plums you have). Place a plum in the centre of each square, then bring up the dough and pinch the edges together to completely seal the plum in the dough.

5 Bring a large pan of water to the boil, and add the dumplings in batches of about six at a time. Cook for about 8 minutes, or until they rise to the surface. Remove with a slotted spoon, transfer to a bowl and keep warm while you cook the remaining dumplings.

6 Heat the remaining butter in a large frying pan, add the breadcrumbs and fry for a few minutes, until golden brown. Add the dumplings and gently turn in the breadcrumbs to coat.

7 Transfer to a warm plate and dust with icing sugar and cinnamon.

Serves 4–6
675g/1½lb potatoes, peeled
250ml/8fl oz/1 cup sour cream
75g/3oz/6 tbsp butter
2 eggs, beaten
250g/9oz/2¼ cups plain (all-purpose) flour, plus extra for dusting
8–12 plums
90g/3½oz/¾ cup icing (confectioners') sugar
30ml/2 tbsp ground cinnamon
45ml/3 tbsp fresh breadcrumbs
icing (confectioners') sugar and cinnamon, for dusting

These traditional sweet dumplings, made with a potato dough, contain a whole plum, stuffed with cinnamon sugar. They are served everywhere in Poland during the autumn.

Honey and Almond Cookies
Pierniki z migdałami

Makes 20

225g/8oz/1 cup clear honey
4 eggs, plus 2 egg whites
350g/12oz/3 cups plain (all-purpose) flour
5ml/1 tsp bicarbonate of soda (baking soda)
2.5ml/½ tsp freshly grated nutmeg
2.5ml/½ tsp ground ginger
2.5ml/½ tsp ground cinnamon
2.5ml/½ tsp ground cloves
20 blanched almond halves

1 Beat together the honey and whole eggs until light and fluffy. Sift over the flour, bicarbonate of soda and spices, and beat to combine.

2 Gather the cookie dough into a ball, wrap in clear film (plastic wrap) and chill in the refrigerator for 1 hour or overnight.

3 Preheat the oven to 200°C/400°F/Gas 6. Roll out the dough on a lightly floured surface to a thickness of 5mm/¼ in. Using a 4cm/1½ in cookie cutter, stamp out 20 rounds.

4 Transfer the rounds to two lightly greased baking trays. Beat the egg whites until soft peaks form. Brush the tops of the rounds with the egg white, then press an almond half into the centre of each one.

5 Place in the oven and bake for 15–20 minutes, or until they are a pale golden brown.

6 Remove from the oven and allow to cool slightly before transferring to a wire cooling rack. Leave to cool completely, then serve.

Ancient Slavic tribes used to make cakes with honey, but it wasn't until the arrival of spices like ginger, cinnamon and cloves in the 17th century that Polish people starting making these sweet and delicious little morsels. These delectable spiced honey cookies are traditionally made at Christmas, when they are given to children, although they are also eaten at other times of the year.

Angel's Wings Chrusty

1 Beat the butter and sugar in a large bowl. Add the eggs, flour, bicarbonate of soda, sour cream, salt, honey, Polish spirit, vodka or rum, and the vinegar.

2 Beat to combine thoroughly and to form a smooth dough. Transfer the dough to a lightly floured surface and roll out a long, thin rectangle, 10cm/4in across, to a thickness of 3mm/⅛ in.

3 Cut the dough lengthways into four 2.5cm/1in strips, then cut each of these horizontally, on a slight slant, into pieces about 10cm/4in long.

4 Make a 4cm/1½in lengthways slit in the middle of each strip. Lift the lower end of the pastry and pass it through the slit. Gently pull it through the other side and downwards to create a twist in the pastry.

5 Heat enough oil for deep-frying to 180°C/350°F/Gas 4, then add the pastry strips in batches of two and fry for 5–8 seconds, until they rise to the surface and are golden brown.

6 Remove from the oil immediately, using a slotted spoon, and drain on kitchen paper. Repeat the process with the remaining pastry.

7 Transfer to a serving dish and dust generously with icing sugar.

COOK'S TIPS
• Add a cube of bread to the hot oil to prevent it from spitting while the cookies are cooking.
• These cookies are delicious eaten warm or cold, but for the best flavour and texture they should be eaten on the day they are made.

Serves 4–6

50g/2oz/¼ cup butter, softened
50g/2oz/¼ cup caster (superfine) sugar
3 egg yolks, plus 1 whole egg
250g/9oz/2¼ cups plain (all-purpose) flour, plus extra for dusting
2.5ml/½ tsp bicarbonate of soda (baking soda)
120ml/4fl oz/½ cup sour cream
pinch of salt
30ml/2 tbsp clear honey
45ml/3 tbsp 95 per cent proof Polish spirit or vodka, or rum
15ml/1 tbsp white wine vinegar
vegetable oil, for deep-frying
icing (confectioners') sugar, for dusting

This old Polish recipe for deep-fried pastry strips dusted with sugar is traditionally made on Fat Thursday, the last Thursday before Lent, and at carnivals.

Poppy Seed Cake Makowiec

Serves 6

45ml/3 tbsp sour cream

50g/2oz fresh yeast or 2 packets active dried yeast

400g/14oz/3½ cups strong white bread flour

115g/4oz/1 cup icing (confectioners') sugar, plus extra for dusting

15ml/1 tbsp grated lemon rind

pinch of salt

150g/5oz/10 tbsp butter, melted and cooled

3 eggs, beaten

For the filling

500g/1¼lb/5 cups poppy seeds

200g/7oz/scant 1 cup butter

200g/7oz/1 cup caster (superfine) sugar

115g/4oz/1 cup chopped almonds

30ml/2 tbsp currants

60ml/4 tbsp honey

45ml/3 tbsp finely chopped candied peel

1 vanilla pod (bean)

3 egg whites, lightly beaten

15ml/1 tbsp rum or cognac

1 To make the filling, place the poppy seeds in a fine mesh sieve and rinse in cold water, then pour boiling water over the seeds. Drain, and transfer to a bowl. Cover with boiling water, then soak for 3 hours.

2 Drain the poppy seeds, then grind with a pestle and mortar.

3 Melt the butter in a pan, then add the sugar, almonds, currants, honey and candied peel. Scrape the seeds from the vanilla pod into the mixture along with the poppy seeds, stir to combine, then fry gently for 20 minutes. Remove from the heat, leave to cool, then stir in the beaten egg whites and rum or cognac.

4 To make the dough, mix the cream with the yeast in a bowl. Sift the flour into a large bowl, then stir in the icing sugar, lemon rind and salt.

5 Make a well in the middle of the dry ingredients, then pour in the cooled melted butter, beaten eggs and the yeast mixture. Mix to combine, then turn out on to a lightly floured surface and knead for about 10 minutes, or until smooth and elastic.

6 Roll out the dough to a thickness of about 5mm/¼ in, then spread evenly with the poppy-seed mixture. Roll up the dough to form a loaf shape and place on a greased baking tray. Cover with a clean, damp dish towel and put in a warm place to rise for 45 minutes.

7 About 10 minutes before the end of the rising time, preheat the oven to 190°C/375°F/Gas 5. Pierce the top of the loaf with a large sharp knife, then put in the hot oven and bake for 45–50 minutes, or until golden brown. Leave to cool, then slice and serve lightly dusted with icing sugar .

This dark, dense cake, made from a sweet dough rolled with an aromatic poppy-seed filling, is made throughout the year, but especially at Christmas and Easter.

Easter Pastry Mazurek

1 Sift the flour and icing sugar into a large bowl. Add the softened butter and egg yolks, and mix to make a smooth dough. Form the dough into a ball, cover with clear film (plastic wrap) and chill for 45 minutes.

2 Preheat the oven to 220°C/425°F/Gas 7. Grease a rectangular baking tray. Roll out the pastry and cut a piece that is the same size as the tray. Place on the tray.

3 Cut the remaining pastry into strips about 1cm/½ in wide and join together to make one long strip. Lightly brush a little water around the edge of the pastry rectangle. Twist the strip of pastry and place over the moistened edge.

4 Bake the pastry in the oven for about 20 minutes, or until golden brown. Leave to cool slightly, then carefully lift it out and cool completely.

5 To make the filling, pour the cream into a heavy pan, then add the sugar and vanilla pod. Gently bring to the boil, then boil for about 5 minutes, stirring constantly, until the mixture is thick.

6 To test whether it is ready, spoon a small amount on to a cold plate. It should set quickly. Remove from the heat and leave to cool slightly.

7 Remove the vanilla pod, then beat in the butter while the cream mixture is still warm. Spread the mixture inside the pastry case, smoothing the top. While the filling is still warm, decorate the top with almonds and dried fruits.

Consumed in vast quantities at Easter, there are many different toppings for these sweet, decorative pastries, including nut paste, almonds, cheese, jams, raisins and coloured icing. This version is made with a rich vanilla cream and studded with almonds and dried fruit.

Serves 6

300g/11oz/2⅔ cups plain (all-purpose) flour
115g/4oz/1 cup icing (confectioners') sugar
250g/9oz/generous 1 cup butter, softened
4 egg yolks

For the filling

500ml/17fl oz/2¼ cups double (heavy) cream
400g/14oz/2 cups caster (superfine) sugar
1 vanilla pod (bean)
400g/14oz/1¾ cups butter
about 150g/5oz each of almonds and dried fruits, to decorate

Apricot Purée with Almonds Morelowy deser

Serves 6

350g/12oz/½ cup dried apricots,
finely chopped
60ml/4 tbsp water
50g/2oz/¼ cup caster (superfine)
sugar
90ml/6 tbsp 95 per cent proof Polish
spirit
75g/3oz/½ cup blanched almonds,
chopped
75g/3oz/½ cup chopped candied
peel
whipped cream and ground
cinnamon, to serve

*Many traditional Polish
desserts are made with
dried fruits, such as plums,
apricots or apples, because
it was once difficult to buy
the fresh variety out of
season. This rich apricot
purée is warming and
nutritious, making it
especially popular during
the winter.*

1 Place the chopped apricots and the water in a heavy pan, bring to
the boil and simmer for 25 minutes.

2 Add the sugar and simmer for a further 10 minutes, or until you have
a thick jam-like mixture.

3 Remove from the heat and stir in the Polish spirit, almonds and candied
peel.

4 Spoon into serving dishes or glasses and leave to cool, then chill in
the refrigerator for at least 2 hours. Just before serving, decorate with
whipped cream and dust with cinnamon.

Nutritional Notes

Sorrel Soup with Eggs: Energy 162kcal/673kJ; Protein 9.8g; Carbohydrate 5g, of which sugars 2g; Fat 11.7g, of which saturates 5g; Cholesterol 205mg; Calcium 215mg; Fibre 2.2g; Sodium 238mg.

Red Borscht Soup: Energy 109kcal/456kJ; Protein 5g; Carbohydrate 13.2g, of which sugars 12.4g; Fat 4.4g, of which saturates 2g; Cholesterol 77mg; Calcium 62mg; Fibre 3.8g; Sodium 121mg.

Potato Pancakes: Energy 291kcal/1221kJ; Protein 6g; Carbohydrate 35.4g, of which sugars 2.9g; Fat 15g, of which saturates 2.2g; Cholesterol 63mg; Calcium 36mg; Fibre 2.1g; Sodium 42mg.

Grilled Sardines with Parsley: Energy 327kcal/1362kJ; Protein 35g; Carbohydrate 0.3g, of which sugars 0.3g; Fat 20.5g, of which saturates 8g; Cholesterol 16mg; Calcium 192mg; Fibre 0.5g; Sodium 240mg.

Halibut Steaks with Lemon Butter: Energy 464kcal/1928kJ; Protein 38.2g; Carbohydrate 0.6g, of which sugars 0.5g; Fat 34.3g, of which saturates 20.1g; Cholesterol 141mg; Calcium 83mg; Fibre 0.6g; Sodium 337mg.

Fried Carp in Breadcrumbs: Energy 479kcal/2008kJ; Protein 32.3g; Carbohydrate 32g, of which sugars 0.9g; Fat 25.6g, of which saturates 4.1g; Cholesterol 148mg; Calcium 133mg; Fibre 1g; Sodium 301mg.

Chicken Casserole: Energy 285kcal/1196kJ; Protein 38.3g; Carbohydrate 6.7g, of which sugars 1.8g; Fat 9.7g, of which saturates 4.5g; Cholesterol 219mg; Calcium 43mg; Fibre 0.8g; Sodium 148mg.

Roast Duck with Fruit Stuffing: Energy 468kcal/1983kJ; Protein 43.5g; Carbohydrate 54.1g, of which sugars 54.1g; Fat 13.7g, of which saturates 2.6g; Cholesterol 220mg; Calcium 99mg; Fibre 7.8g; Sodium 241mg.

Wild Boar with Sweet-and-sour Sauce: Energy 655kcal/2734kJ; Protein 73g; Carbohydrate 17.4g, of which sugars 8.8g; Fat 33g, of which saturates 12.5g; Cholesterol 228mg; Calcium 63mg; Fibre 3.3g; Sodium 578mg.

Roast Beef Roll: Energy 360kcal/1510kJ; Protein 50.1g; Carbohydrate 2.9g, of which sugars 0.8g; Fat 16.6g, of which saturates 8g; Cholesterol 177mg; Calcium 23mg; Fibre 0.3g; Sodium 267mg.

Breaded Pork Cutlets: Energy 591kcal/2475kJ; Protein 55.9g; Carbohydrate 34.9g, of which sugars 0.9g; Fat 26.2g, of which saturates 5.6g; Cholesterol 237mg; Calcium 92mg; Fibre 1.3g; Sodium 317mg.

Hunter's Stew: Energy 546kcal/2279kJ; Protein 50.4g; Carbohydrate 24.6g, of which sugars 19.8g; Fat 26.4g, of which saturates 9.7g; Cholesterol 149mg; Calcium 213mg; Fibre 7.7g; Sodium 2122mg.

Stuffed Cabbage Rolls: Energy 414kcal/1725kJ; Protein 27.6g; Carbohydrate 28.7g, of which sugars 8.2g; Fat 21g, of which saturates 8.5g; Cholesterol 126mg; Calcium 99mg; Fibre 3.4g; Sodium 133mg.

Sautéed Wild Mushrooms: Energy 303kcal/1253kJ; Protein 5.5g; Carbohydrate 13.7g, of which sugars 8.4g; Fat 25.6g, of which saturates 15.8g; Cholesterol 69mg; Calcium 98mg; Fibre 2.8g; Sodium 125mg.

Spiced Red Cabbage: Energy 112kcal/469kJ; Protein 2g; Carbohydrate 17.1g, of which sugars 15.5g; Fat 2.4g, of which saturates 1.3g; Cholesterol 5mg; Calcium 55mg; Fibre 3.1g; Sodium 25mg.

Potato and Cheese Dumplings: Energy 419kcal/1768kJ; Protein 11.7g; Carbohydrate 71.6g, of which sugars 2.3g; Fat 11.5g, of which saturates 2.9g; Cholesterol 100mg; Calcium 136mg; Fibre 3.1g; Sodium 57mg.

Mashed Potato Dumplings: Energy 313kcal/1321kJ; Protein 7.5g; Carbohydrate 56g, of which sugars 2.8g; Fat 8.1g, of which saturates 4.4g; Cholesterol 48mg; Calcium 69mg; Fibre 2.8g; Sodium 240mg.

Buckwheat Kasha: Energy 180kcal/746kJ; Protein 2.9g; Carbohydrate 25.7g, of which sugars 0g; Fat 7.8g, of which saturates 0.9g; Cholesterol 0mg; Calcium 10mg; Fibre 0g; Sodium 0mg.

Apple and Leek Salad: Energy 59kcal/252kJ; Protein 1.9g; Carbohydrate 12.5g, of which sugars 11.8g; Fat 0.6g, of which saturates 0.1g; Cholesterol 0mg; Calcium 27mg; Fibre 3.4g; Sodium 4mg.

Beetroot Salad: Energy 60kcal/253kJ; Protein 1.5g; Carbohydrate 9g, of which sugars 8.5g; Fat 0.1g, of which saturates 0g; Cholesterol 0mg; Calcium 20mg; Fibre 1.6g; Sodium 221mg.

Polish-style Cucumber Salad: Energy 48kcal/196kJ; Protein 1.1g; Carbohydrate 1.8g, of which sugars 1.7g; Fat 4.1g, of which saturates 2.5g; Cholesterol 12mg; Calcium 31mg; Fibre 0.4g; Sodium 10mg.

Polish Cheesecake: Energy 347kcal/1448kJ; Protein 10.8g; Carbohydrate 24.8g, of which sugars 21.6g; Fat 23.6g, of which saturates 13.4g; Cholesterol 196mg; Calcium 34mg; Fibre 0g; Sodium 131mg.

Plum Dumplings: Energy 510kcal/2147kJ; Protein 11.1g; Carbohydrate 72.6g, of which sugars 18.6g; Fat 21.6g, of which saturates 12.4g; Cholesterol 115mg; Calcium 147mg; Fibre 5.3g; Sodium 190mg.

Honey and Almond Cookies: Energy 112kcal/473kJ; Protein 3.4g; Carbohydrate 22.6g, of which sugars 8.9g; Fat 1.5g, of which saturates 0.4g; Cholesterol 38mg; Calcium 33mg; Fibre 0.5g; Sodium 22mg.

Angel's Wings: Energy 364kcal/1527kJ; Protein 7.7g; Carbohydrate 45.7g, of which sugars 14g; Fat 16.2g, of which saturates 8.3g; Cholesterol 203mg; Calcium 104mg; Fibre 1.3g; Sodium 79mg.

Poppy Seed Cake: Energy 1302kcal/5437kJ; Protein 21.9g; Carbohydrate 124.4g, of which sugars 72.9g; Fat 83.2g, of which saturates 35.9g; Cholesterol 224mg; Calcium 438mg; Fibre 6.6g; Sodium 459mg.

Easter Pastry: Energy 1989kcal/8270kJ; Protein 14.9g; Carbohydrate 149.4g, of which sugars 110.6g; Fat 152.2g, of which saturates 86.5g; Cholesterol 480mg; Calcium 270mg; Fibre 4g; Sodium 703mg.

Apricot Purée with Almonds: Energy 230kcal/973kJ; Protein 5.1g; Carbohydrate 38.3g, of which sugars 37.9g; Fat 7.4g, of which saturates 0.6g; Cholesterol 0mg; Calcium 93mg; Fibre 5.2g; Sodium 46mg.

Index